A+
MY REPORT

HAPPY BIRTHDAY!

A+
MY REPORT

HAPPY BIRTHDAY!

HAPPY BIRTHDAY

HAPPY BIRTHDAY

MOVING
VAN
INC.
ST

MOVING VAN
INC.
ST

PRINCIPAL

PRINCIPAL

BUS
STOP

CAT IN THE
DR. SEUSS

BUS STOP

DR. SEUSS
CAT IN THE

E THEATE
NOW PLAYING
NOW PLAYING
NOW PLAY

E THEATE
NOW PLAYING
NOW PLAYING
NOW PLAY